LAB LAUGHS!

SCIENCE JOKES FOR KIDS

—— KEVIN & WALLY CLUNE ——

DEDICATION

For

mommy

TABLE OF CONTENTS

PARENTS / TEACHERS

The purpose of this book is to introduce a wide variety of scientific topics to young readers, while doing so in a silly and engaging way. After each joke you will find a fact or description that helps to add context to these topics, written in a style that we hope children will better comprehend. In these paragraphs, we use metaphors and otherwise not-so scientific language to explain complex concepts, which may at times seem like a stretch from the literal definitions found in textbooks. We hope that this is an effective way of opening up imaginations to let in these new thoughts and ideas that can otherwise seem boring or confusing.

CHAPTER 1
PLANETS &
SOLAR SYSTEM

Did you hear about the moon that went crazy?

What a "lunar-tic!" 😂

☽ **Moons:** Can you believe that some moons have their own moons? They are called moonmoons or submoons. Just like Earth has a moon, some of those moons have tiny moons circling around them. It's like a little family in space!

~~~~~~

Why did the sun need a vacation?

It was feeling a little "burned out!" 🤪

☼ **Sun:** The Sun is so big that you could fit almost 1.3 million Earths inside of it! Imagine a giant beach ball with a bunch of tiny marbles inside. And even though it's so far away, it gives us light and warmth every day, making life possible here on Earth.

~~~~~~

How do comets wash themselves?

They take a "meteor shower!" 🤭

✳ **Comets:** Meteor showers are like nature's fireworks. When Earth passes through the tail of a comet, tiny bits of the comet burn up in our atmosphere, creating bright streaks in the sky. So, when you see a meteor shower, you're actually watching pieces of an ancient comet's tail!

What did the alien say to the bird?
"Take me to your feeder!" 😎

👀 **Aliens:** The word "alien" doesn't just mean little green creatures from outer space! The word originally comes from the Latin word "alienus," which means "foreign" or "stranger."

〜〜〜〜

How does Saturn get in touch with Jupiter?
It "gives it a ring!" 😄

🪐 **Saturn:** Did you know that Saturn is so light that if you could find a swimming pool big enough, it would actually float on the water? That's because the entire planet is mostly made of gas!

〜〜〜〜

Why did the telescope break up with the microscope?
They just couldn't "see things on the same scale." 🤪

🔭 **Telescopes:** Telescopes are like super-powers for your eyes! With big telescopes the size of a school bus, we can see stars that are billions of miles away. Imagine being able to see an ant on the moon!

Why aren't black holes invited to birthday parties?
They "suck the fun" out of everything! 🤣

◎ **Black Hole**: Did you know that black holes are like giant cosmic vacuum cleaners? They suck up everything close to them, even light. But don't worry, the nearest one is way too far away to bother Earth.

~~~~~~

What was the astronomer's nickname on his diving team?
The "big dipper!" 😎

🐻 **Constellations:** The Big Dipper isn't its own constellation. It's part of a bigger constellation called Ursa Major, which means "Big Bear." So, when you look up at the Big Dipper, you're actually looking at the bear's tail and part of its body!

~~~~~~

Why did the astronaut leave the galaxy?
To take a "space-cation!" 😄

📱 **Galaxies:** Our Milky Way galaxy is so big that even if you could travel on a super-fast spaceship going the speed of light, it would still take you over 100,000 years to get from one side to the other!

WORD SEARCH 1

```
A  H  T  H  O  W  U  M  O  Y  C  X
T  T  S  G  G  A  J  W  T  O  V  E
M  E  C  L  A  W  W  I  O  W  B  N
O  L  G  O  L  L  V  W  T  M  R  Z
S  E  A  P  M  A  A  T  W  U  M  S
P  S  V  S  R  E  E  X  T  Q  O  T
H  C  T  G  T  K  T  A  Y  D  O  A
E  O  F  Q  C  E  S  G  U  V  N  R
R  P  A  O  J  X  R  H  E  R  O  D
E  E  R  M  E  T  E  O  R  F  V  U
P  B  F  Y  W  G  H  T  I  Z  M  S
A  S  T  R  O  N  A  U  T  D  H  T
```

ASTEROID	ASTRONAUT	ATMOSPHERE
COMET	GALAXY	GRAVITY
METEOR	MOON	ROCKET
SATURN	STARDUST	TELESCOPE

ou call it when the
re gets grumpy?

ir-ritated!" 🤪

Atmosphere: Did you know that Earth's atmosphere is like a big, invisible blanket? It keeps our planet warm, protects us from harmful sun rays, and is the reason we can breathe and fly kites. Thank you, atmosphere!

∿∿∿∿

How do astronauts put their babies to sleep?

They "rock-et!" 🚀

🚀 **Rocket:** Rockets work in space because they push out gas really fast from the bottom, which makes the rocket move in the opposite direction. It's like when you blow up a balloon and let it go — it zooms all over the place!

∿∿∿∿

Why did the astronaut sneeze in space?
She was "allergic to stardust!" 😎

☀ **Stardust:** Did you know that everything on Earth (including you), is made from stardust? A long time ago, giant stars exploded, scattering dust and gas which later came together to form our planet and everything on it.

Why the astronomer miss spotting
the shooting star?

Because he just "couldn't focus!" 😄

⭐ **Meteor:** When a meteor zooms through the sky
and we see a bright streak of light, we sometimes call
it a "shooting star." But guess what? It's not really a
star at all! It's just a chunk of space rock burning up
in our atmosphere.

〰️〰️〰️

I used to tell a great joke about gravity...

...but it just "never landed." 🤪

♀ **Gravity:** If there was no gravity, we'd float away
like balloons! It's gravity that keeps our feet on the
ground and makes things fall. So next time you drop
your ball or toy, you can thank gravity for bringing it
down and not out to space!

〰️〰️〰️

Why can't satellites talk to each other?
The conversation always "goes
in circles." 😵

🛰️ **Satellites:** Satellites are like space detectives!
They orbit high above the Earth and can take
pictures of our planet, help our phones and TVs
work, and even track the weather for us.

How does the moon cut its hair?
"E-clipse it!" 😎

🌑 **Eclipse:** An eclipse is like a cosmic game of peek-a-boo! Sometimes the Moon sneaks in front of the Sun, and we get a solar eclipse. Other times, Earth's shadow hides the Moon, and we see a lunar eclipse.

~~~~~~

Where do astronauts keep their teacups?
On "flying saucers!" 😄

🛸 **UFOs:** "UFO" is just a short way of saying "Unidentified Flying Object." It doesn't always mean aliens; it just means something in the sky that we can't identify. So, a balloon or a toy drone might be a UFO until we know what it is.

~~~~~~

What do astronauts use to keep their pants up?
An "asteroid belt!" 😵

☄️ **Asteroid Belt:** Did you know that the asteroid belt is like a giant obstacle course located between the orbits of Mars and Jupiter? It's filled with rocky and metallic objects tumbling around in space.

ANSWER KEY 1

A	H	T	H	O	W	U	M	O	Y	C	X
T	T	S	G	G	A	J	W	T	O	V	E
M	E	C	L	A	W	W	I	O	W	B	N
O	L	O	L	L	V	W	T	M	R	Z	
S	E	A	P	M	A	A	T	W	U	M	S
P	S	V	S	R	E	E	X	T	Q	O	T
H	C	T	G	T	K	T	A	Y	D	O	A
E	O	F	Q	C	E	S	G	U	V	N	R
R	P	A	O	J	X	R	H	E	R	O	D
E	E	R	M	E	T	E	O	R	F	V	U
P	B	F	Y	W	G	H	T	I	Z	M	S
A	S	T	R	O	N	A	U	T	D	H	T

ASTEROID	ASTRONAUT	ATMOSPHERE
COMET	GALAXY	GRAVITY
METEOR	MOON	ROCKET
SATURN	STARDUST	TELESCOPE

What do you get when you shoot off fireworks in space?

A "big bang!" 🌀

🎉 **Big Bang Theory:** Did you know that the Big Bang Theory is like the ultimate birthday party for the universe? Scientists believe that 13.8 billion years ago, everything we see in the sky and even our planet started from a tiny, super-hot point and then exploded outwards.

~~~~~~

What do NASA engineers roast on the campfire?

"Mars-shmallows!" 😎

🗼 **Mars:** Did you know that the planet Mars has the tallest volcano in the entire solar system? It's called "Olympus Mons," and it's almost as big as the entire state of Arizona!

~~~~~~

How do astronauts refer to the International Space Station?

Their "satellite office!" 😄

📺 **Space Station:** Can you believe that astronauts on the International Space Station (ISS) see 16 sunrises and sunsets every day? That's because the ISS orbits the Earth once every 90 minutes!

Why did the photon get pulled over?

It was moving at the "speed of light!" 😵

🏃 **Speed of Light:** Did you know that the speed of light is so fast that if you could travel at that speed, you could fly around the Earth over 7 times in just one second? That's super-speedy!

~~~~~~

Why did the space explorer
visit Neptune?

He heard it had "great atmosphere!" 😵

🗓 **Neptune:** A year on Neptune is crazy-long! It takes Neptune 165 Earth years to go around the Sun just once. So, if you lived on Neptune, you'd have to wait a really, really long time for your birthday to come around again!

~~~~~~

Why did the bird decide to fly to space?

He thought he saw a "wormhole!" 😎

🐌 **Wormholes:** A wormhole is like a magical tunnel in space. If they really exist, you could enter one end and pop out somewhere completely different in the universe, almost like a shortcut through space!

CHAPTER 2
CHEMISTRY & EXPERIMENTS

What do you call an acid that's always angry?

"A-mean-o!" 😂

🧱 **Amino Acids:** Amino acids are like the building blocks for our body. Just like how LEGO pieces can be put together to make all sorts of shapes and models, our body uses amino acids to build proteins that help us grow, move, and stay healthy.

〰〰〰〰

Why do scientists make great comedians?

They know how to "get a reaction!" 🤪

🧪 **Chemical Reactions:** When you mix baking soda and vinegar, it creates a bubbly reaction just like a mini volcano! This is because the baking soda (a base) and the vinegar (an acid) react to produce carbon dioxide gas. That's why it bubbles up!

〰〰〰〰

How often did hydrogen bump into oxygen?

"Periodically!" 🤣

⚛ **Hydrogen:** When two tiny hydrogen atoms team up with one bigger oxygen atom, they create a water molecule! That's why water's secret code name is H_2O. So, every time you drink a glass of water, you're sipping on billions of these tiny teams.

Why do test tubes love to party?

Because they always "mix things up!" 😎

🔖 **Test Tubes:** A test tube is like a tiny glass tunnel that's closed at one end and open at the other. Scientists use it to mix different liquids and see what happens. It's like a little container where you can watch science experiments come to life!

~~~~~

Did you hear about the beaker that finished school?

It was a "graduated" cylinder! 😄

🥤 **Beakers:** Both a beaker and a graduated cylinder are like measuring cups for scientists! They use them to measure liquids super accurately in their experiments. So, next time you see one, think of it as a scientist's special cup for cooking up cool discoveries.

~~~~~

Why did the gas go to anger management?

Because it was always "fuming!" 😵

👃 **Gasses:** Did you know that methane, a gas found in cow burps and farts, can be used as a source of energy? Some farms even collect this gas to help power their operations. That means that if you hear a cow moo, they might be making electricity!

What did the gas say to the solid?
"Lighten up" already! 😵

😵 **Solids:** Solids have a superpower where they can keep their shape all by themselves! Unlike liquids that need a container or gases that spread out everywhere, solids stand strong and stay in one shape. It's like they're playing a never-ending game of "freeze tag."

~~~~~~

Why did the atoms become best friends forever?
Because they really "bonded!" 😎

⚛ **Atom:** Did you know that everything around you is made up of atoms? Sometimes, they come together and 'stick' to each other, forming a bond. This is like how friends hold hands or give each other a hug.

~~~~~~

What did the chemist say when he found two isotopes of helium?
"HeHe!" 😄

♀ **Helium:** Helium (He) is a gas that can make your voice sound funny and high-pitched. This is because when you breathe it in, it is lighter than the air in your lungs. But always remember, it's just for fun and not safe to breathe in too much!

WORD SEARCH 2

```
K  L  X  V  R  Q  N  S  M  V  Y  I
U  M  A  B  P  W  G  U  E  S  D  S
K  O  W  S  O  J  I  A  L  J  B  O
D  L  R  N  E  L  Y  T  E  T  E  T
Y  E  E  F  E  R  Z  O  C  E  A  O
U  C  A  H  P  Q  L  M  T  S  K  P
R  U  C  M  S  X  S  C  R  T  E  E
A  L  T  K  O  N  O  Q  O  T  R  T
N  E  I  T  A  N  L  M  N  U  K  E
I  A  O  G  E  B  I  P  S  B  S  A
U  Y  N  V  E  O  D  X  F  E  E  V
M  S  C  I  E  N  T  I  S  T  Z  O
```

ATOM   BEAKER   ELECTRONS
HELIUM   ISOTOPE   LASER
MOLECULE   REACTION   SCIENTIST
SOLID   TEST TUBE   URANIUM

What is a scientist's favorite nursery rhyme?

"Hot-cross buns-en!" 😵

💧 **Bunsen Burner:** The Bunsen burner, a tool used in science labs to heat things up, was named after a German scientist named Robert Bunsen. He helped design it to make a flame that scientists could control really well, so they could do experiments safely. It's like a special science candle!

~~~~~~

What do you call a molecule that is always cracking jokes?

A "gas!" 🤣

⚗️ **Molecules:** Just like how a drawing is made up of different colors of crayons, everything around us is made up of different kinds of molecules. And just like you can't see individual crayon marks without looking closely, we can't see individual molecules without a microscope!

~~~~~~

Why doesn't carbon ever go to practice?

It's a "natural!" 😎

♣ **Carbon:** In science, elements like carbon are called "natural elements" because they are found in nature and aren't made by humans. We use these elements in everyday things. For example, the tip of your pencil is a form of carbon called graphite!

Why don't electrons get along with neutrons?
Everything always "revolves around them!" 😄

⚡ **Electrons:** In an atom, electrons move around the nucleus in paths called orbits. They are so tiny that if you lined them up, it would take about 2.5 million of them to make a line as thick as a single strand of human hair!

~~~~~~

What do you call an atom that is always cold?
An "ice-o-tope!" 🤪

👯 **Isotope:** An 'isotope' is like a twin in the world of atoms. Just like twins can look the same but have different personalities, isotopes of an element have the same number of protons but different numbers of neutrons. It's like having siblings with the same last name but different first names.

~~~~~~

Why does uranium listen to music?
Because it's "radio-active!" 🤭

☢️ **Uranium:** Uranium is a metal that can sometimes glow in the dark. It's used as fuel for some power plants and is always kept safely contained. Imagine a metal that could light up like a glow stick!

Why did the manometer take a day off?
It was under "too much pressure!" 😎

🔖 **Pressure:** A manometer is like a special ruler that measures the push of air or gas (called pressure). Just like how we can measure how tall you're getting, a manometer can tell us how strong the air is pushing.

~~~~~~

What is tungsten's favorite type of music?

"Heavy metal!" 😂

🎷 **Tungsten:** Tungsten has the highest melting point of all the elements on the periodic table! It's so strong that it can stay solid even when it's super hot, like the temperature inside a lava lamp. That's why they sometimes use it for the tiny wire inside light bulbs!

~~~~~~

How can you tell when a laser is happy?
They're "beaming from end-to-end!" 😲

⊗ **Lasers:** "Laser" (or LASER) is a short way of saying "Light Amplification by Stimulated Emission of Radiation." It's like a magic light that can be super focused! Some lasers are even used to play music and videos on round discs called CDs and DVDs.

ANSWER KEY 2

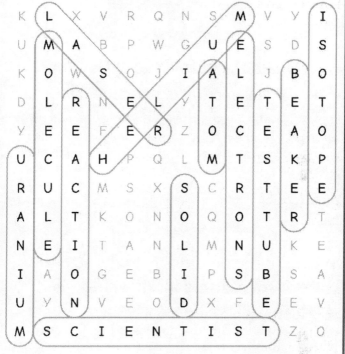

K	L	X	V	R	Q	N	S	M	V	Y		I
U	M	A	B	P	W	G	U	E	S	D		S
K	O	W	S	O	J	I	A	L	J	B		O
D	L	R	N	E	L	Y	T	E	E	E		T
Y	E	E	F	E	R	Z	O	C	E	A		O
U	C	A	H	P	Q	L	M	T	S	K		P
R	U	C	M	S	X	S	C	R	T	E		E
A	L	T	K	O	N	O	Q	O	T	R		T
N	E	I	T	A	N	L	M	N	U	K		E
I	A	O	G	E	B	I	P	S	B	S		A
U	Y	N	V	E	O	D	X	F	E	E		V
M	S	C	I	E	N	T	I	S	T	Z		O

ATOM	BEAKER	ELECTRONS
HELIUM	ISOTOPE	LASER
MOLECULE	REACTION	SCIENTIST
SOLID	TEST TUBE	URANIUM

What did sodium say to potassium?
"I've got my ion you!" 🤩

🔋 **Ions:** An "ion" is like a tiny particle that has either lost or gained an electron, making it charged. It's like when you rub a balloon on your hair and it sticks to the wall – that's because of charges, just like ions.

~~~~~~

Why did the particle go to therapy?
It was feeling "unstable!" 😎

⚗️ **Particles:** Stable particles are like the superheroes of the tiny particle world. They don't change or break apart, no matter how much time passes. Just like how your favorite toy stays the same when you aren't using it, these particles stay the same forever.

~~~~~~

What did the pipette say to the scientist?
"Ex-squeeze me for dripping!" 😄

💧 **Pipette:** A pipette is like a tiny straw scientists use to move very small amounts of liquid from one place to another. Imagine using a straw to pick up just one drop of juice – that's what scientists can do with a pipette!

Where do crystals take their lunch break?

At the "food quartz!" 😜

💎 **Crystals:** Crystals are like nature's puzzles. They grow in special patterns that fit together perfectly, just like pieces of a jigsaw puzzle. Some crystals, like sugar and salt, are even in the foods we eat.

〜〜〜〜

Why did the metalloid join the orchestra?

It made a "great conductor!" 🤣

🪨 **Metalloid:** Did you know that silicon, a metalloid, is found in sand and is used to make computer chips? So, the same stuff you build sandcastles with at the beach is also used to power your video games!

〜〜〜〜

What is big, round, and made of iron?

A "ferrous wheel!" 😎

⚙ **Iron:** 'Ferrous' is a fancy word that means something contains iron. So, if you have a toy truck made of ferrous metal, it has iron in it. And guess what? A magnet will stick to it because magnets love iron!

CHAPTER 3
COMPUTERS & ROBOTICS

Why do robots always call home? To "connect with their motherboard!" 😄

🏢 **Motherboard:** A motherboard is like the "big city" inside your computer where all the other parts live. Just like how roads connect houses and buildings in a city, the motherboard connects things like the brain (CPU), memory (RAM), and even the "post office" (hard drive) of your computer.

〜〜〜〜

Why did the robot get booed at the improv?

Because all his jokes were "scripted!" 🤪

🎬 **Automation:** An automation script is like a magical spell for computers. Just like how a wizard uses a spell to make something happen, an automation script tells a computer exactly what steps to take to complete a task all by itself.

〜〜〜〜

Why did the programmer take a day off? Because she just "couldn't function!" 🤭

🎮 **Programmer:** Did you know that computer programmers are the people that make video games come to life? They write special instructions (called functions) that tell the computer how to make characters move, jump, and even talk in the game!

How do you make a robot angry?

You keep "pressing his buttons." 😎

⚙️ **Robotics:** In car factories, large robot arms that help to build vehicles move in such a coordinated way that it looks like they're dancing. These robot arms can weld, install parts, and even lift heavy objects, all while moving together like dancers on a stage!

~~~~~

Why did the hard drive get a stomach-ache?

It had too many "bytes to eat." 😄

📚 **Hard Drive:** A single hard drive can hold more information than a whole library full of books. One gigabyte, a unit used to measure storage space, can hold about 1,000 thick books worth of text!

~~~~~

Why are search engines so good at dancing?

They have great "algo-rhythm!" 😵

🎲 **Algorithms:** An algorithm is like a recipe for a computer. Just like how a recipe tells you step-by-step how to make cookies, an algorithm tells a computer step-by-step how to solve a problem or do a task.

Why do developers always use credit cards?

Because they "run out of cache!" 😵‍💫

✦ **Cache:** A cache is like a secret treasure chest for a computer! Just like pirates hide their gold and jewels in a treasure chest to find them quickly later on, a computer stores important information in a "cache" so it can find and use it as fast as possible the next time it needs it.

〰〰〰

What's a flower's favorite subject?

"STEM!" 😎

🌱 **STEM:** The word "STEM" is like a code word. It stands for "Science, Technology, Engineering, and Math!" People started using this special code word to talk about these four subjects all together because they help us solve problems, build cool things, and understand the world around us!

〰〰〰

How did HTML break up with CSS?

She said "I want a DIV-orce!" 😄

🦴 **HTML:** Did you know that in the world of computer coding, HTML is like the skeleton of a webpage, CSS is the design, and DIVs are like the building blocks? Just like you use blocks to build a tower, programmers use DIVs to stack, arrange, and organize things on a website.

WORD SEARCH 3

```
P  Y  J  A  V  A  S  C  R  I  P  T
I  D  I  D  M  J  Y  K  M  Q  Y  M
J  X  V  D  O  E  U  H  I  S  G  O
A  X  B  A  H  E  T  X  E  T  G  T
J  Z  X  C  H  I  K  N  S  E  R  H
Z  F  A  T  R  T  O  Q  S  M  O  E
M  C  H  O  V  R  M  W  X  I  B  R
X  I  G  H  D  I  B  L  W  P  O  B
F  L  A  P  T  O  P  K  I  B  T  O
A  U  T  O  M  A  T  I  O  N  I  A
B  L  O  C  K  C  H  A  I  N  C  R
B  A  T  T  E  R  I  E  S  U  S  D
```

ALGORITHM   AUTOMATION   BATTERIES
BLOCKCHAIN   CACHE   DRONE
HTML   JAVASCRIPT   LAPTOP
MOTHERBOARD   ROBOTICS   STEM

Why did the robot always drink coffee?
He was written in "java-script!" 😵

○ **JavaScript:** JavaScript is like the "magic wand" of websites. It helps to make websites interactive, like letting you play games or chat with friends online, all without having to leave the webpage!

~~~~~~~

Why did the IT department hire a flight attendant?
To put a "server in the cloud!" 😵

☁ **Cloud Computing:** Cloud servers are like super-strong computers that live far away but can send information to your computer really quickly. They help you watch videos, play games, and save your pictures without taking up space on your own phone or computer!

~~~~~~~

What do you call a flying pastry?
A "drone-ut!" 😎

☗ **Drones:** Some drones are even used by farmers to help take care of their crops. These special drones can fly over fields and take pictures to show which plants need more water or are sick. It's like having a flying helper on the farm!

What did big data say to little data?
"Wanna grab a byte?" 😄

🧩 **Big Data:** 'Big data' is like a giant toy box filled with millions of pieces! Scientists and computer experts use special tools to put these pieces together to create and discover amazing new things.

〰〰〰

Why do jails get such great 5G reception?
They always have "full bars!" 😵

📶 **Mobile Networks:** Did you know that 5G is like a super-fast invisible train that carries information to and from our phones and devices? It's so speedy that it can download a whole movie, app or game in just a few seconds!

〰〰〰

Why did the website fail the math test?
It just wasn't his "domain!" 🤪

🌐 **Domains:** Domain names are like the addresses for websites on the internet! Just like how every house has a unique address, every website has a unique domain name. If you ever want to visit a website, you can just type in the domain address and go there.

Why did the autonomous car break-up with its driver?

He was "too controlling!" 😎

🚙 **Self-Driving Cars:** Did you know that self-driving cars have special 'eyes' called sensors? These sensors help the car see the road, other cars, and even people, so it can drive all by itself without a human driver!

~~~~~~

Why couldn't the LaserJet make the 3D printer laugh?

Because all his jokes "fell flat!" 😂

🏰 **3D Printing:** 3D printing is like building a sandcastle, but instead of using a bucket and sand, it uses a special machine and material like plastic. The machine adds one tiny layer of material at a time, stacking them up until it creates a whole object, just like you stack layers of sand to make a castle!

~~~~~~

How do you comfort a video game?

You "console it!" 😜

🕹 **Video Games:** The very first video game (called "Tennis for Two") wasn't made on a computer or a gaming console like we have today. It was actually created in 1958 on a huge machine almost as big as a refrigerator!

ANSWER KEY 3

```
P  Y  (J  A  V  A  S  C  R  I  P  T)
I  D  I  D  M  J  Y  K  M  Q  Y  M
J  X  V  D  O  E  U  H  I  S  G  O
A  X  B  A  H  E  T  X  E  T  G  T
J  Z  X  C  H  I  K  N  S  E  R  H
Z  F  A  T  R  T  O  Q  S  M  O  E
M  C  H  O  V  R  M  W  X  I  B  R
X  I  G  H  D  I  B  L  W  P  O  B
F  (L  A  P  T  O  P)  K  I  B  T  O
A  U  T  O  M  A  T  I  O  N  I  A
B  L  O  C  K  C  H  A  I  N  C  R
B  A  T  T  E  R  I  E  S  U  S  D
```

ALGORITHM   AUTOMATION   BATTERIES
BLOCKCHAIN   CACHE   DRONE
HTML   JAVASCRIPT   LAPTOP
MOTHERBOARD   ROBOTICS   STEM

Why did the humanoid stay home from school?

It "caught a virus!" 🤒

🤖 **Humanoid:** Humanoid robots are robots that are designed and built to act like people. They can walk on two legs, wave hello, and some can even dance!

〰〰〰

What is a zoologist's favorite programming language?

"Python!" 😎

🐍 **Python:** Python programming language is not named after a snake! The person who came up with it named it after a TV show called "Monty Python's Flying Circus" because it was fun and easy to read.

〰〰〰

Why did the lithium battery take a nap?
It needed to "recharge!" 😂

🔋 **Batteries:** Did you know that lithium is used to make batteries that power things like your toys, phones, and even electric cars? But guess what? It's also the lightest metal and can float on water!

How did the VR gamer avoid
getting attacked?

He "took off his glasses!" 😜

👓 **Virtual Reality**: Virtual reality (VR) is like a magic trick for your eyes and ears. When you put on a VR headset, it shows you pictures so quickly that your brain thinks you're really inside a video game or a faraway place!

〰〰〰〰

Why did the blockchain developers go to
peer mediation?

They just couldn't "hash it out!" 🤭

📓 **Blockchain:** Think of a blockchain like a magic notebook that everyone can see. Each new note in the notebook gets a unique sticker called a "hash." If even one word changes, the sticker changes too, so everyone knows that the change was made safely and securely.

〰〰〰〰

Did you hear about the laptop that
lost his temper?

He really "flipped his lid!" 😎

💻 **Laptop:** The first laptop computer was called the "Osborne 1," and it was as big as a suitcase. It was invented by a man named Adam Osborne in 1981. Imagine carrying that to school every day!

CHAPTER 4
EARTH &
GEOLOGY

Why don't fossils like scary movies?
They're "petrifying!" 😄

🦕 **Fossils:** Did you know that fossils are like nature's time capsules? When plants or animals get buried quickly by mud or sand, over millions of years, their remains can turn into stone through a process called petrification.

~~~~~

Why don't sedimentary rocks get cold in the winter?

They always "dress in layers!" 🤪

📖 **Sedimentary:** Sedimentary rocks are like a scrapbook! They're made from tiny bits of other rocks, plants, and even animal shells that pile up over time. If you look closely, you might find clues about what the Earth was like a long, long time ago!

~~~~~

Why did the volcano join the gym?

It was trying to "stay active!" 🌋

🌋 **Volcano:** Did you know that when a volcano erupts, it can create new land? In Hawaii, there's a volcano called Kilauea, and its eruptions have added about 500 acres of land to the island over the past 30 years!

Why did the lava need some sleep?
It was "having a meltdown!" 😎

🪨 **Lava:** Did you know that when lava cools down and hardens, it can form rocks? Some of these rocks are so light and full of air bubbles that they can float on water like a rubber duckie! They're called "pumice stones."

~~~~~~

Why does lodestone have so many friends?
Its personality is "magnetic!" 😄

🧲 **Magnetic:** There's a special rock called "lodestone" that acts like a natural magnet. Long before we had fancy compasses, sailors used these rocks to help them find their way at sea because they always point towards the North and South poles!

~~~~~~

How do earthquakes make promises?
They "shake on it!" 😵

🌋 **Earthquakes:** Earthquakes are like the Earth's way of saying 'excuse me!' when it needs to stretch and move. Just like when we wiggle around to get comfy, the Earth does too, and that's when we feel a shake!

Why does the earth's core never pay attention?

Because he's too "deep in thought!" 🌍

🌑 **Earth's Core:** Did you know that the Earth's core is so hot that it's hotter than the surface of the Sun? It's like having a huge, fiery ball right in the center of our planet, keeping us warm and generating a protective magnetic field around the Earth.

~~~~~~

What did the tectonic plate say when it collided with another?

"Oops, my fault!" 😎

🧩 **Tectonic Plates:** Earth's surface is a lot like a big jigsaw puzzle. These puzzle pieces are called tectonic plates, and they move around very slowly. Sometimes, when they bump into each other, it can cause earthquakes!

~~~~~~

Why did the pebble get in trouble at school?

Because it kept "skipping!" 😄

🔵 **Pebbles:** Pebbles are like toy marbles formed by nature! They start as big rocks, and over time, water and wind wear them down into the smooth, round stones we find at the beach or riverbanks.

WORD SEARCH 4

```
P  T  N  F  L  W  O  M  W  W  F  Y
L  E  R  O  S  I  O  N  H  B  W  O
A  M  G  S  V  O  L  C  A  N  O  M
T  I  C  S  M  R  C  V  C  J  C  G
E  N  E  I  K  U  N  U  A  M  L  C
A  E  X  L  M  H  O  B  V  F  A  L
U  R  W  S  G  W  E  R  E  A  V  H
F  A  S  O  I  L  U  K  V  B  A  P
J  L  Z  G  L  A  C  I  E  R  E  U
D  S  Q  K  M  A  G  N  E  T  I  C
E  L  I  M  E  S  T  O  N  E  G  Y
S  E  D  I  M  E  N  T  A  R  Y  T
```

CAVE	EROSION	FOSSILS
GLACIER	LAVA	LIMESTONE
MAGNETIC	MINERALS	PLATEAU
SEDIMENTARY	SOIL	VOLCANO

What did the slate say to the limestone?
Don't "take me for granite!" 😵

🪨 **Limestone:** Limestone can be made from ancient sea creatures like shells and corals that piled up over millions of years! And granite is like nature's confetti, made of tiny bits of different minerals that sparkle and shine.

~~~~

What is a coal miner's favorite place to eat?

The "Hard Rock Cafe!" 😵

⛏ **Mining:** Did you know that coal is often called "black gold"? Long ago, when dinosaurs roamed the Earth, plants that died turned into coal over millions of years. Today, miners dig deep underground to find this "black gold" and use it to make electricity!

~~~~

How do you know when you are trapped in quicksand?

You get a "sinking feeling!" 😎

📽 **Quicksand:** While quicksand looks scary in the movies, it is usually not deep enough to swallow a person completely in real life. The human body is also less dense than quicksand so it's even possible to float on top of it. Just don't try this yourself!

Where do geologists keep their books?
On the "mantle!" 😄

🐾 **Mantle:** Did you know that Earth's mantle is like a super thick layer of gooey caramel in the middle of a candy planet? Imagine the Earth as a giant jawbreaker candy, and the mantle is the squishy part in the middle!

~~~~~~

What did the permafrost say to the glacier?

"Ice to meet you!" 😵

❄ **Glacier:** Glaciers are like giant slow-moving rivers of ice. Some of them can take hundreds of years to move just a few miles. Imagine a snail racing a glacier – believe it or not, the snail might actually win!

~~~~~~

What do minerals do when they get their paycheck?

They make a "deposit!" 💿

💎 **Minerals:** Mineral deposits are like Earth's jewelry box! Over time, the Earth collects and stores minerals in special places called deposits. Some of these minerals sparkle and shine, and we use them to make jewelry, like gold and diamonds.

Why did the excavator decide to take a nap?

Because it finally "hit bedrock!" 😎

🏠 **Bedrock:** Did you know that bedrock is like the Earth's "basement"? It's the solid rock layer beneath all the soil and sand. Just like a basement is at the bottom of a house, bedrock is at the bottom of the ground we walk on!

~~~~~~

What did the cliff say to the ocean?

"You are really wearing me down!" 😄

🪨 **Erosion:** Can you believe that Erosion is like nature's way of redecorating? Over time, wind and water can move soil and rocks from one place to another, changing the shape of landscapes. Sometimes, it can take thousands of years for erosion to shape hills, valleys, and coastlines.

~~~~~~

Why did the geyser take up yoga?

She needed to "blow off steam!" 😵

💧 **Geyser:** Did you know that a geyser is like Earth's natural water fountain? It shoots up hot water and steam from underground because of heated rocks! Some geysers can even shoot water higher than a 10-story building!

ANSWER KEY 4

P	T	N	F	L	W	O	M	W	W	F	Y
L	E	R	O	S	I	O	N	H	B	W	O
A	M	G	S	V	O	L	C	A	N	O	M
T	I	C	S	M	R	C	V	C	J	C	G
E	N	E	I	K	U	N	U	A	M	L	C
A	E	X	L	M	H	O	B	V	F	A	L
U	R	W	S	G	W	E	R	E	A	V	H
F	A	S	O	I	L	U	K	V	B	A	P
J	L	Z	G	L	A	C	I	E	R	E	U
D	S	Q	K	M	A	G	N	E	T	I	C
E	L	I	M	E	S	T	O	N	E	G	Y
S	E	D	I	M	E	N	T	A	R	Y	T

CAVE   EROSION   FOSSILS
GLACIER   LAVA   LIMESTONE
MAGNETIC   MINERALS   PLATEAU
SEDIMENTARY   SOIL   VOLCANO

Why do penguins love the polar ice cap?
It's a "great place to chill!" 🫠

😊 **Ice Cap:** Can you believe that the polar ice caps are like Earth's giant air conditioners? They reflect sunlight back into space, helping to keep our planet cool. It's like we are wearing a big sun hat to stay cool!

~~~~~~~

Why did the tide sign up for CrossFit?
He was trying to "get ripped!" 😎

🌊 **Tide:** Did you know that tides are caused by the gravitational pull of the moon and the sun on Earth's oceans? It's like they're playing a gentle game of tug-of-war with the water! Sometimes, water rushes quickly back out to sea in what's called a riptide.

~~~~~~~

What did the soil say to the seed?
"I'm rooting for you!" 😄

🍰 **Soil:** Soil is like a giant cake made of tiny ingredients. It has bits of rocks, dead plants, and even tiny animals. And just like a cake has different layers, soil does too. Each layer tells a story about the Earth's history!

Why don't stalactites go out to parties?
They prefer to "hang at home!" 😜

😶 **Caves:** Did you know that stalactites are like nature's icicles hanging from the ceiling of caves? They grow super slowly, only about an inch every 100 years. So, if you see a long stalactite, it's like looking at a piece of ancient artwork made by dripping water!

~~~~~

Why did the plateau decide to retire?
It was "past its peak!" 😵

🏞 **Plateau:** A plateau is like a giant table standing on the earth. It's a flat area high above the ground, like a mountain with a flat top. Sometimes, people call plateaus the "stairs of the earth" because they look like steps leading up to the sky.

~~~~~

Why is it so easy to trick a gorge?
Because he "falls for it" every time! 😎

💦 **Waterfall:** Did you know that a gorge is also like a giant natural staircase for rivers? When a river flows down a steep slope, it can carve out a deep, narrow valley called a gorge. And sometimes, when the river takes a big step down, it creates a waterfall!

CHAPTER 5
WEATHER & CLIMATE

How does thunder listen to music?

It uses a "boombox!" 😄

✋ **Thunder:** Thunder is caused by lightning. When lightning strikes, it heats up the air around it so quickly that the air expands and creates a loud BOOM! It's like nature's way of clapping!

〜〜〜〜

Did you hear about the guy that was struck by lightning?

He was "shocked!" 😵

⚡ **Lightning:** Did you know that a bolt of lightning can be five times hotter than the surface of the Sun? When it strikes sandy areas, the intense heat can even melt the sand and form a special kind of glass called 'fulgurite'!

〜〜〜〜

What is a tornado's favorite dance move?

The "twist!" 😵‍💫

🌪 **Tornados:** Did you know that tornadoes can spin as fast as race cars zoom around the track? Some tornadoes can whirl around at speeds of up to 300 miles per hour. But unlike racecars, tornadoes can also hop and skip across the ground.

Why did La Niña break up with El Niño?
He was too "hot and cold!" 😎

😵 **El Niño / La Niña:** 'El Niño' and 'La Niña' are like the ocean's mood swings! Sometimes the Pacific Ocean gets warmer (El Niño) and sometimes it gets cooler (La Niña). Just like how our moods can change the way we act, these changes can affect weather all around the world!

∿∿∿∿

What did the hurricane say to the palm tree?
"Hang in there!" 😂

◉ **Hurricanes:** Did you know that the middle of a hurricane is called the "eye"? And even though hurricanes are super stormy, the eye is calm and can even have clear skies! It's like the quiet center of a spinning top.

∿∿∿∿

Where does the sun like to surf?
On a "heat wave!" 🥴

🔍 **Heat Wave:** Did you know that during a heatwave, the air can get so hot that it can fry an egg on the sidewalk? It's like the Earth is turning into a giant frying pan! But remember, it's always safer to cook your eggs on the stove with a grown-up's help.

What do clouds say when they have a bad day?

"Don't worry, it'll blow over." 🌀

🌑 **Clouds:** Clouds can have funny names based on their shapes. One of these is called a "cumulus" cloud, which looks like fluffy, white cotton balls floating in the sky. Even though they look light and fluffy, a single cumulus cloud can weigh as much as 100 elephants!

~~~~~~

Why is fog so easy to get along with?

It's "down-to-earth!" 😎

🏚 **Fog:** Did you know that fog is like a cloud that has come down to visit the ground? It's made up of lots of tiny water droplets floating in the air, just like clouds. So, when you walk through fog, you are walking through a cloud!

~~~~~~

Why did the meteorologist break up with the news anchor?

She kept "stealing his thunder!" 😄

🔬 **Meteorologist:** Meteorologists are just like detectives! They look for clues in the weather to solve mysteries about what the sky is going to do next. They use cool gadgets and tools to measure things like temperature, wind, and even how much water is in the air.

WORD SEARCH 5

```
Z  L  E  H  A  V  A  L  A  N  C  H  E  R
M  T  H  U  N  D  E  R  C  M  G  D  T  H
C  V  G  I  V  R  E  Y  J  N  D  M  Y  U
V  L  M  G  F  Y  D  P  P  R  A  F  G  R
A  R  O  N  D  Q  U  T  A  W  G  M  L  R
K  D  Z  U  W  O  N  Z  O  N  H  I  C  I
G  R  R  G  D  L  Z  B  I  R  A  V  E  C
H  O  E  A  T  I  N  N  Z  H  N  Q  K  A
A  U  Q  D  L  I  T  P  Y  U  U  A  F  N
Q  G  Y  B  A  H  K  Y  R  F  Q  M  D  E
Y  H  Z  R  G  C  N  A  V  G  Q  J  J  O
X  T  E  I  S  A  N  D  S  T  O  R  M  T
A  A  L  R  U  B  L  C  D  Z  D  N  G  R
M  E  T  E  O  R  O  L  O  G  I  S  T  G
```

AVALANCHE	BLIZZARD	CLOUD
DROUGHT	HAIL	HURRICANE
LIGHTNING	METEOROLOGIST	RAINBOW
SANDSTORM	THUNDER	TORNADO

What do you call a lost dog in a snowstorm?

A "pup-sicle!" 😵

❄ **Snowstorms:** Did you know that each snowflake in a snowstorm is unique? They all have their own special shape and design, like tiny pieces of art falling from the sky! When they all come together, they create a big, fluffy blanket of snow.

〰〰〰

Why did the leaf decide to fall off the tree?

It wanted to "branch out!" 🍃

🍂 **Autumn:** In autumn, trees like maple and oak change colors because they stop making a green pigment called chlorophyll. Without it, other hidden colors like red, orange, and yellow get their chance to shine!

〰〰〰

What did summer say to spring?

"I'm just getting warmed up." 😎

☺ **Summer:** In the summer, the days are longer because the Earth tilts towards the sun. That's why we get more sunlight, and it feels warmer. So, summer is like Earth's way of giving us extra playtime outside!

Why couldn't the snowman keep any friends?

Because he was "too flaky!" 😂

❄ **Winter:** Did you know that the world's largest snowman was built in Maine, USA, in 2008? It stood at an impressive 122 feet and 1 inch tall. That's as tall as a 10-story building! Imagine how many snowballs it took to make that giant snowman.

〜〜〜〜

Why did the weatherman bring a towel to work?

He was "calling for showers!" 🤪

❀ **Spring:** Did you know that in spring, flowers and trees wake up from their long winter's nap and start to grow again? It's like nature's way of throwing a big, colorful party with lots of beautiful flowers and baby animals joining in on the fun!

〜〜〜〜

What did the tsunami say to the typhoon?

Nothing, it just "waved!" 🤭

🌊 **Tsunami:** The word "tsunami" is actually two Japanese words put together. "Tsu" means harbor and "Nami" means wave. So, it's like calling it a "harbor wave"! But remember, even though the name sounds cool, tsunamis can be destructive.

Why doesn't hail ever catch a cold?
It always stays "ice-o-lated!" 😎

🌩 **Hail:** Hailstones start as tiny ice pellets in thunderstorms and grow bigger as they get tossed up and down in the cloud, collecting more layers of ice. It's like they're playing dress-up, adding more and more icy coats!

〜〜〜〜

How does a leprechaun hunt for gold?
With a "rain-bow!" 😄

🌈 **Rainbow:** Rainbows are like giant circles in the sky, but we usually only see half of them because the ground is in the way. If you're ever in an airplane or on a mountaintop, you might be lucky enough to see a full circle rainbow!

〜〜〜〜

Why is the dew point so hard to predict?
Because it's too "mist-erious!" 🤪

🌫 **Mist**: In tropical rainforests, sometimes after a heavy rainstorm, a magical mist rises from the ground. This is nature's way of keeping the forest cool and giving it that mysterious, fairy-tale look!

ANSWER KEY 5

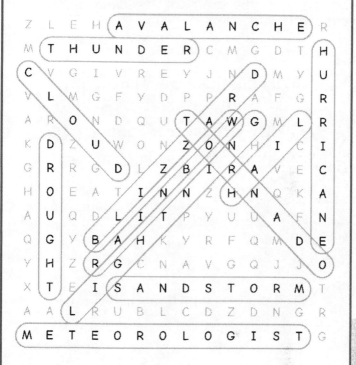

Z L E H A V A L A N C H E R

M T H U N D E R C M G D T H

C V G I V R E Y J N D M Y U

V L M G F Y D P P R A F G R

A R O N D Q U T A W G M L R

K D Z U W O N Z O N H I I I

G R R G D L Z B I R A V E C

H O E A T I N N Z H N Q K A

A U Q D L I T P Y U U A F N

Q G Y B A H K Y R F Q M D E

Y H Z R G C N A V G Q J J O

X T E I S A N D S T O R M T

A A L R U B L C D Z D N G R

M E T E O R O L O G I S T G

AVALANCHE   BLIZZARD   CLOUD
DROUGHT   HAIL   HURRICANE
LIGHTNING   METEOROLOGIST   RAINBOW
SANDSTORM   THUNDER   TORNADO

What did the tree say to the wind?
"Leaf me alone!" 🌀

🍃 **Wind:** Did you know that wind is invisible, and we can only see its effects on things like trees swaying, leaves rustling, or a flag fluttering? It is created when the sun heats the Earth unevenly, causing the air to move around.

〰〰〰

Why did the farmer laugh at the drought?
He had a "dry sense of humor!" 😎

💤 **Drought:** During a drought, some plants can 'take a nap' and go dormant to save water. Just like how bears hibernate in winter, these plants will pause their growth and wait for the rain to come back. When the rains return, they "wake up" and start growing again!

〰〰〰

What's a blizzard's favorite game to play?
"Freeze tag!" 😄

❄ **Blizzard:** A blizzard is like a snowstorm's big brother. For it to be called a blizzard, the snowstorm must have winds over 35 mph and reduce visibility to less than a quarter mile for at least 3 hours!

What do you call a blackout in the middle of the day?

A "power nap!" 😜

🕯 **Blackout:** In big cities with lots of lights, it's hard to see the stars at night because of something called 'light pollution'. But during a blackout, when all the lights go out, the stars can shine super bright! It's like nature's own light show!

~~~~~

Did you hear about the tumbleweed that made it across the country?

It was "blown away!" 🤣

🌀 **Tumbleweed:** Did you know that tumbleweeds are actually plants? When they're done growing, they dry up, break off from their roots, and the wind rolls them around like big, bouncy balls, spreading their seeds everywhere they go!

~~~~~

How does a snowman survive an avalanche?

He just "rolls with it!" 😎

🏔 **Avalanche:** An avalanche is like a giant snow slide! When too much snow piles up on a mountain, it can suddenly come rushing down super-fast. While it may look exciting, it's important for people to stay safe and keep their distance.

CHAPTER 6.
ANIMALS & INSECTS

Why did the cat wear a fancy coat?
Because it was "feline fabulous!" 😂

🐱 **Cats:** Cats have a special reflective layer behind their eyes! This layer helps them see better in the dark. It's also the reason why cat's eyes can appear to glow when light shines on them, like little headlights!

~~~~~~

What's a flying squirrel's favorite sport?
"Hang gliding," of course! 😵

🐿 **Flying Squirrels:** Flying squirrels don't "fly" like a robin or a cardinal would. They actually just glide through the air using a special flap of skin called a "patagium" that stretches from their wrists to their ankles. It's like they have their own built-in parachute!

~~~~~~

Why do giraffes have long necks?
So they can't smell their feet! 😝

🦒 **Giraffes:** Did you know that a giraffe's tongue can be up to 20 inches long? That's almost as long as an adult's arm! They use their long tongues to grab leaves from tall trees and even to clean their own ears.

What happened to the snake that ate the poison dart frog?

He "croaked!" 😎

🐸 **Poison Dart Frogs:** Poison dart frogs are so colorful because their bright patterns warn predators that they are toxic and not a tasty snack. But don't worry, when they're raised in captivity without their natural diet, they don't produce their famous poison!

~~~~~~

What do hermit crabs do when they find a new home?

They "shell-ebrate!" 😂

🦀 **Hermit Crabs:** Hermit crabs are like the original house hunters. They don't grow their own shells, so as they get bigger, they must find a new, larger shell to move into. It's like they're playing musical chairs!

~~~~~~

Why did the shark cross the road?

To get to the "other tide!" 🤪

🦈 **Sharks:** Did you know that some sharks can glow when it is dark? The swell shark and the chain catshark have special patterns on their skin that light up in deep, dark waters. It's like they have their own underwater nightlights!

What do you call a sea-cow that is always poking fun?

A "mana-tease." 🐂

🐄 **Manatee:** Manatees are sometimes called 'sea cows' because they graze on underwater plants, just like cows munch on grass in a field! But don't be fooled by their size; they're gentle giants and can swim gracefully through the water.

〰〰〰

What do rhinos do when they are stuck in traffic?

They "lay on the horn!" 😎

🦏 **Rhinoceros:** Did you know that a rhinoceros's horn is made of the same material as our hair and nails? It's called keratin! Unlike other animals with hard horns or antlers made of bone, a rhino's horn grows throughout its life just like our fingernails do.

〰〰〰

Why did the chickadee join the gym?

He wanted to "work on his pecks!" 😄

🍔 **Chickadees:** Did you know that chickadees have a special song that sounds like they're saying 'cheeseburger'? Next time you hear one, listen closely and see if you can hear them ordering their favorite snack.

WORD SEARCH 6

```
K  C  S  W  O  R  D  F  I  S  H  H
A  Z  C  H  A  M  E  L  E  O  N  E
N  E  G  M  H  H  J  A  F  M  H  R
G  Y  X  A  U  D  V  N  L  A  E  M
A  X  S  T  I  T  E  T  A  N  U  I
R  T  L  U  T  Q  B  E  M  A  V  T
O  Z  Q  A  G  B  Y  A  I  T  M  C
O  S  C  R  K  I  D  T  N  E  N  R
S  N  L  P  H  Z  S  E  G  E  S  A
F  T  H  R  O  I  M  R  O  H  T  B
E  Y  P  A  N  D  A  O  E  F  O  X
L  H  O  D  A  S  P  I  D  E  R  H
```

ANTEATER	CAT	CHAMELEON
FLAMINGO	FOX	HERMIT CRAB
KANGAROO	MANATEE	PANDA
SPIDER	SQUID	SWORDFISH

What do you call a reptile that solves mysteries?
An "investi-gator!" 😵

🐊 **Alligators:** Did you know that alligators have a "built-in" navigation system? They have a special ability to find their way home even if they are moved far away from their original location. Scientists believe they use the Earth's magnetic field, like a natural GPS.

〰〰〰

Why did the squid ask for a pencil?
Because he "ran out of ink!" 🤭

🦑 **Squid:** Can you believe that when a squid gets scared, it shoots out ink like a superhero using a smoke screen? This inky cloud confuses predators and gives the squid a chance to escape. What a cool trick!

〰〰〰

What is a seagull's favorite dip?
"Squawk-amole!" 😎

🐦 **Seagull:** Did you know that seagulls can drink both fresh and saltwater? They have special glands near their eyes that help filter out the salt, which they then "sneeze" out through their nostrils!

Why did the fox cross the road?

He was following the chicken! 😂

🦊 **Fox:** Can you believe that foxes use their tails not only for balance but also to keep warm during cold nights? They wrap it around themselves, just like we might use a cozy scarf or our favorite blanket.

〜〜〜〜〜

What do you call a buck that can't see?
"No eye-deer!" 😵

🦌 **Deer:** Deer have a special stomach with four parts! It's like they have four mini-stomachs inside one big one. This helps them digest tough plants and leaves. Imagine if you had four stomachs – think of all the ice cream you could eat!

〜〜〜〜〜

How do turtles talk to each other from across the pond?

They use their "shell-phones!" 🐢

🐢 **Turtles:** Did you know, some turtles can breathe through their butts? It's true! These turtles have a special part in their rear called a 'cloaca' that allows them to take in oxygen when they're underwater. It's like they have a secret snorkel on their backside!

Where do spiders shop for shoes?
On the "web!" 🤪

🕷 **Spider:** Did you know that some spiders can actually "fly"? They release thin silk threads that catch the wind, allowing them to float through the air for long distances. It's like they have their own little parachutes!

~~~~~

What is an anteater's favorite fish?
An "ant-chovy!" 😎

🐜 **Anteater:** Can you believe that anteaters don't have any teeth? Instead, they use their long, sticky tongues, which can be up to 2 feet long, to slurp up thousands of ants and termites every day!

~~~~~

What type of bird can you see in the dark?
A "flamin-glow!" 😄

🦩 **Flamingo:** Flamingos are actually born with gray feathers, not pink ones! It's their diet of brine shrimp and blue-green algae that turns them pink as they grow up. They are living proof of the saying, "you are what you eat!"

ANSWER KEY 6

```
K  C  S  W  O  R  D  F  I  S  H  H
A  Z  C  H  A  M  E  L  E  O  N  E
N  E  G  M  H  H  J  A  F  M  H  R
G  Y  X  A  U  D  V  N  L  A  E  M
A  X  S  T  I  T  E  T  A  N  U  I
R  T  L  U  T  Q  B  E  M  A  V  T
O  Z  Q  A  G  B  Y  A  I  T  M  C
O  S  C  R  K  I  D  T  N  E  N  R
S  N  L  P  H  Z  S  E  G  E  S  A
F  T  H  R  O  I  M  R  O  H  T  B
E  Y  P  A  N  D  A  Q  E  F  O  X
L  H  O  D  A  S  P  I  D  E  R  H
```

ANTEATER	CAT	CHAMELEON
FLAMINGO	FOX	HERMIT CRAB
KANGAROO	MANATEE	PANDA
SPIDER	SQUID	SWORDFISH

Did you hear about the panda that lost all his money?

He got "bamboozled!" 😵

🐼 **Panda:** Pandas love to munch on bamboo so much that they can eat it for up to 12 hours a day. That's like eating breakfast, lunch, and dinner over and over again! They even have a special thumb that helps them grab and eat it easily.

~~~~~~

Why don't chameleon's throw birthday parties?

They are just trying to "blend in!" 🦎

🦎 **Chameleon:** Did you know that chameleons have special eyes? Each eye can move by itself, which means they can look in two different directions at the same time. Imagine being able to watch your favorite show and play a board game at the same time!

~~~~~~

What do you call a group of whales that play instruments?

An "orca-stra!" 😎

🐋 **Orcas / Dolphins:** Orcas, also known as "killer whales," are not actually whales! They are the largest member of the dolphin family. Despite their nickname, they are very playful and smart, and they can even learn to communicate with humans.

Which animals are great at fencing?
"Swordfish!" 😄

✎ **Swordfish:** Swordfish are super speedy swimmers. They can zoom through the water at speeds of up to 60 miles per hour! That's as fast as a car on a highway. Their long, pointy "swords" help them slice through the water quickly.

~~~~~

What do bees use to brush their hair?
A "honey-comb!" 😵

🐝 **Bees:** Did you know, bees make honeycombs in a hexagon shape because it's the most efficient way to fill space without any gaps, while using the least amount of wax? It's like nature's perfect shape!

~~~~~

Why aren't raccoons allowed in restaurants?
Because of their "trashy" behavior! 🤭

🦝 **Raccoon:** Raccoons have five fingers just like humans and are very good at using their hands. They can open jars, untie knots, and sometimes even wash their food before eating it. Even though they get a bad reputation, raccoons are very smart and play an important role in our ecosystem.

CHAPTER 7
PLANTS & HABITATS

How did Tarzan learn to travel by jungle vines?

He "took a swing at it!" 😄

🦶 Jungle: Did you know that in the jungle, there are plants called 'walking trees'? They can actually 'move' by growing new roots in the direction they want to go and letting old ones die off.

〰〰〰

How do you pack for a picnic in the desert?

Make a "sand-wich!" 🤪

🏜 Desert: Can you believe that if you took all the sand from every desert in the world and spread it out, it would cover the entire United States with a layer about 1 foot deep! That's one big sandbox!

〰〰〰

Why does coral primarily live in tropical waters?

They find it "reef-freshing!" 🐠

🐡 Coral Reefs: Just like how cities have lots of different buildings and people, coral reefs have thousands of different types of fish and creatures living together. Some fish even have cleaning stations (like a car wash), where tiny fish nibble away dirt and parasites!

Why couldn't the young plant photosynthesize?

It was too "green!" 😎

🍳 **Photosynthesis:** Did you know that during photosynthesis, plants are like little green chefs? They take ingredients like sunlight, water, and carbon dioxide to cook up their own food, and as a special treat, they create oxygen for us to breathe!

~~~~~~

Why did the dandelion lose the beauty pageant?

They were "weeding out" the competition! 😂

🌼 **Dandelion:** Even though many people consider dandelions to be weeds, they can be used in making salads and teas. They can also tell time! In the morning, dandelion flowers open up to greet the sun, and in the evening, they close to say goodnight.

~~~~~~

Why don't pinecones watch romantic comedies?

They are too "sappy!" 😵

🔺 **Pinecones:** Did you know that pinecones can act like weather forecasters? When it's dry and sunny, they open, but when it's going to be rainy, they close tight to protect their seeds.

How do oak trees access social media?
They "log" in! 🤳

🌳 **Oak:** Did you know that there are over 600 different species of oak trees around the world? Some oak trees have leaves with smooth edges, while others have leaves with wavy or spiky edges. And their acorns come in all sorts of shapes and sizes too!

〰〰〰〰

Why can't one mountain hear the others talking?
It was "out-of-range!" 😎

⛰ **Mountains:** Some mountains are so tall that they actually poke through the clouds! And in some mountain ranges, the tops of the mountains are covered in snow all year round, even in summer. That's like having winter at the top and summer at the bottom at the same time!

〰〰〰〰

Why couldn't the ranger get a job in the Outback?
He wasn't "koala-fied!" 😄

🐨 **Australian Outback:** In the Australian Outback, there are termite mounds so tall that they can be as high as a two-story building! These tiny termites create a network of tunnels and chambers inside, much like architects building skyscrapers.

WORD SEARCH 7

```
D  E  S  E  R  T  D  I  P  E  K  Y
G  J  P  I  N  E  C  O  N  E  B  I
O  S  L  W  I  V  V  S  W  A  M  P
C  E  U  R  J  O  U  T  B  A  C  K
A  R  I  M  U  S  H  R  O  O  M  U
C  E  S  C  A  C  T  U  S  A  G  E
O  N  T  O  K  P  N  O  T  Q  X  I
R  G  P  Z  J  U  N  G  L  E  M  V
N  E  V  M  O  U  N  T  A  I  N  M
X  T  G  F  O  U  L  K  J  W  D  W
W  I  L  D  F  L  O  W  E  R  J  F
O  C  O  R  A  L  R  E  E  F  S  N
```

ACORN	CACTUS	CORAL REEF
DESERT	JUNGLE	MOUNTAIN
MUSHROOM	OUTBACK	PINECONE
SERENGETI	SWAMP	WILDFLOWER

Where do parrots sleep in the rainforest?

A "canopy" bed! 😲

🐖 **Rain Forest:** Did you know that the world's rainiest jungle is called the Chocó rainforest in Colombia? It gets so much rain that if you left a bucket outside for a year, it would fill up with over 500 inches of water!

~~~~~~

Did you hear about the guy that fell into the hot spring?

He was "steaming!" 😵‍💫

🛁 **Hot Springs:** Hot springs are like nature's bathtubs! They're warm and steamy because water from deep underground gets heated up by hot rocks, then bubbles up to the surface. Some animals even like to take a dip in them to stay warm when it's cold!

~~~~~~

Why don't animals play poker in the Serengeti?

Too many "cheetahs!" 😎

🐐 **Serengeti:** The Serengeti isn't just grasslands! It's like a giant patchwork quilt made of different landscapes, including woodlands, swamps, and even rivers. Over a million wildebeests march across it every year in a big parade called the Great Migration.

Why didn't the dinosaur have to decorate?

His house was "fully fern-ished!" 😄

🪴 **Ferns:** Ferns have been around for more than 300 million years! That's way before the dinosaurs roamed the Earth. Unlike many plants, ferns don't have flowers or seeds. Instead, they reproduce by tiny spores that can be carried by the wind.

〰〰〰

Why do bats love cactus flowers?

Because they are "succulent!" 😵

🌵 **Cacti:** Did you know that some bats are like late-night gardeners for cacti? When it is dark, these bats sip nectar from cactus flowers and, in return, help spread pollen so the cactus can produce fruit. It's a sweet partnership in the desert!

〰〰〰

Why did the venus flytrap start eating snails?

It was cutting back on "fast food!" 😵

🪰 **Venus Fly Trap:** Did you know that the Venus fly trap has a way of "counting"? It can sense how many times an insect touches its inner hairs. After two touches, SNAP! It closes its trap in hopes of catching the insect.

Why can't mushrooms predict the weather?

It's too "spore-adic!" 😎

🍄 **Mushrooms:** When mushrooms "open up" like an umbrella, they release tiny seeds called spores. A single mushroom can release billions of these spores. Much like a magical fairy dust that can float on a breeze and start new mushrooms far, far away!

~~~~~~

What did the fungus say when he raced the algae!

"I'm lichen my chances!" 😄

◎ **Lichens:** Lichens are like nature's best buddies. They're made of two different organisms – a fungus and an algae – living together in a special partnership. It's like they're holding hands and helping each other survive in some of the toughest places on Earth!

~~~~~~

What did the beach say to the jetty?
"Long-tide, no see!" 😵

🏖 **Beaches:** Did you know that jetties, those long structures you see sticking out into the water at the beach, are like traffic directors? They are placed there to control the movement of sand and water, just like traffic lights control cars on the road!

ANSWER KEY 7

```
D  E  S  E  R  T  D  I  P  E  K  Y
G  J  P  I  N  E  C  O  N  E  B  I
O  S  L  W  I  V  V  S  W  A  M  P
C  E  U  R  J  O  U  T  B  A  C  K
A  R  I  M  U  S  H  R  O  O  M  U
C  E  S  C  A  C  T  U  S  A  G  E
O  N  T  O  K  P  N  O  T  Q  X  I
R  G  P  Z  J  U  N  G  L  E  M  V
N  E  V  M  O  U  N  T  A  I  N  M
X  T  G  F  O  U  L  K  J  W  D  W
W  I  L  D  F  L  O  W  E  R  J  F
O  C  O  R  A  L  R  E  E  F  S  N
```

ACORN	CACTUS	CORAL REEF
DESERT	JUNGLE	MOUNTAIN
MUSHROOM	OUTBACK	PINECONE
SERENGETI	SWAMP	WILDFLOWER

Why did the wildflower go to college?

To be a "leader in its field!" 🤭

✿ **Wildflower:** Some wildflowers, like snapdragons, have special "landing pads" just for bees and insects. When a bee lands on the flower, it changes color to guide the bee to the yummy nectar inside. While the bee enjoys a treat, the pollen hitches a ride and spreads!

～～～～

How do alligators relax in the swamp?

They take a "mud-bath!" 😎

🌱 **Swamp:** When you walk through a swamp, you might hear little popping or bubbling sounds coming from below your feet. This isn't from swamp creatures, but because swamps are often filled with gases like methane, which is produced when plants decay in the water.

～～～～

What has a bed that you cannot sleep on?

A river! 😄

🎲 **Rivers:** Did you know that riverbeds can be like secret highways for animals? Many creatures, such as fish, otters, and even bears, use riverbeds as paths to travel, find food, and sometimes even to build their homes. So, I guess you can sleep on them after all!

Why were the geese late to the marsh?
They got "bogged down!" 😵

🪨 **Marsh:** Marshes act like giant sponges. When it rains a lot, they soak up all the extra water, which helps to prevent flooding in nearby areas. Plus, all those plants, like cattails and reeds, help clean the water by trapping and breaking down stuff that shouldn't be there!

〜〜〜〜

Why don't acorns need invitations?
They always "drop in" anyway! 😵

🔻 **Acorns:** Did you know that oak trees produce acorns, but not right away? It can take an oak tree up to 20 years before it starts making its very first acorns! And when it does, animals like squirrels, deer, and birds love to eat them.

〜〜〜〜

Why did the beaver give up on the dam?
It was feeling "too drained!" 😎

🏠 **Dams:** Just like humans build dams to control water levels and create reservoirs, beavers do their own construction projects to make a safe and comfy home! This allows them to build these homes, called lodges, in the water where they can stay away from predators.

CHAPTER 8
BIOLOGY &
HUMAN BODY

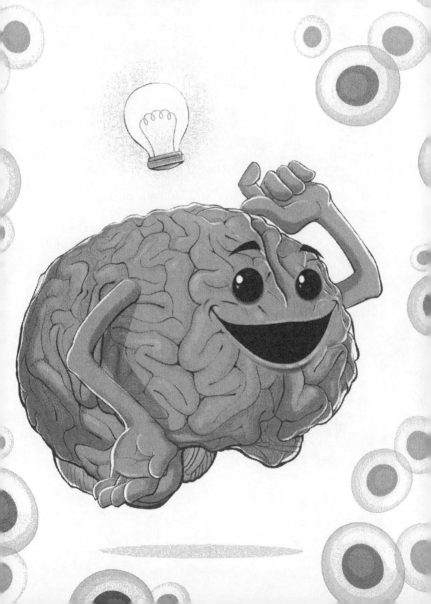

What did one blood cell say to the other?
"B positive!" 😄

🚑 **Blood:** Did you know that your blood type, such as B positive, is like a secret code that tells doctors what kind of blood you can receive if you ever need extra? B+ blood is super special because it can be given to people with B+, B-, O+, and O- blood types!

~~~~~~~

Why doesn't the digestive system watch horror movies?
He just "can't stomach them!" 🤪

🚌 **Digestive System:** Did you know that your digestive system is like a super-long slide that's about 30 feet long from start to finish? If you could lay out your entire digestive system, it would be almost as long as a school bus!

~~~~~~~

My doctor once asked me if my nose was full of mucus...
I told her, "No, it's snot." 🤭

💧 **Mucus:** Mucus wraps around the insides of your nose like a trap to catch tiny invaders (such as germs and dust) before they can make you sick. So, every time you blow your nose, you're actually getting rid of the bad guys that the mucus has caught!

Did you hear about the lung that won the beauty contest?

She was "breath-taking!" 😎

Lungs: Did you know that your lungs are not identical twins? That's right! Your right lung is a bit larger and has three sections, called lobes, while your left lung has only two lobes to make space for your heart.

~~~~~~

Why did the elbows go to the bank?

They had to open a "joint account!" 😂

Elbow: Your elbow is a special kind of joint called a "hinge joint." Just like the hinges on a door allow it to swing open and closed, your elbow hinge lets you swing your forearm up and down. Pretty cool, right?

~~~~~~

Why are skeletons so calm?

Nothing gets "under their skin!" 😨

Bones: When you were born, you had more bones than you do now as an adult. But where'd they go? Babies are born with about 270 bones, but as they grow, some of these bones gradually fuse together. By the time you become an adult, you'll have only 206 bones!

Why do skulls always show up early?
They are trying to get a "head start!" 🤕

💀 **Skull:** Did you know that when you were a baby, your skull had soft spots called 'fontanelles'? These flexible spots allow your brain to grow quickly. As you get older, they slowly close and harden to form your skull.

~~~~~

I asked my ENT if we could talk...
She said "I'm all ears!" 😎

👂 **Ears:** Our ears not only help us hear sounds but also help us keep our balance! Inside our ears, there are tiny stones that move around and tell our brain if we are standing up straight, leaning, or lying down.

~~~~~

Did you hear about the brain that got stuck at the rail station?
He lost his "train of thought." 😂

🧠 **Brain:** Did you know that your brain is like a super-powered computer that never turns off? Every single thought you have creates a tiny electrical zap! These zaps zoom around inside your brain, helping you think, remember, and imagine all sorts of fantastic things.

WORD SEARCH 8

```
U  N  E  R  Y  B  P  I  R  X  X  G
D  X  E  Y  E  B  A  L  L  Q  A  N
A  L  O  M  E  S  T  O  M  A  C  H
R  P  I  Y  B  A  C  T  E  R  I  A
T  B  B  O  N  E  S  F  H  K  R  E
E  K  D  L  U  N  G  S  V  I  G  S
R  I  L  B  R  P  L  G  A  G  U  L
I  D  R  F  R  L  P  H  O  C  Z  C
E  N  K  E  D  A  H  Q  U  I  P  S
S  E  B  A  N  S  I  M  C  D  V  M
G  Y  K  P  A  M  B  N  Y  P  X  U
V  K  L  P  Y  A  Y  V  T  M  A  A
```

ARTERIES   BACTERIA   BONES
BRAIN   DNA   EYEBALL
HAIR   KIDNEY   LUNGS
MUCUS   PLASMA   STOMACH

Why do veins and arteries always fight?
I guess they have "bad blood!" 😵

Arteries: Arteries are like superhighways for your blood! They carry fresh, oxygen-rich blood from your heart to all parts of your body, just like roads help cars get from one place to another. And the biggest artery, called the aorta, is almost as wide as a garden hose!

~~~~~~

Why don't neurons raise their hands in class?
It's too "nerve-wracking!" 😵

Nervous System: Did you know that your nervous system is like your body's own instant messaging service? When you touch something hot, your nerves send a message to your brain almost like a text message, at speeds of up to 250 miles per hour!

~~~~~~

How do stomachs know which friends to trust?
They have a "gut-feeling!" 😎

Stomach: The stomach uses strong acids to help break down the food we eat. These acids are so powerful that they could even dissolve metal! So, to protect itself, the stomach constantly renews its lining, creating a brand new one every 3-4 days.

Did you hear about the finger that won the cooking competition?

It was a "nail-biter!" 😂

🖌 **Fingernails:** Did you know that your fingernails grow faster when you're asleep? While we snooze, our body works hard repairing and growing our cells, including the ones in our nails. This is why it's so important to get a good night's sleep!

~~~~~

What did the plasma say when it rang the doorbell?

"Anti-body home?" 🤪

◐ **Plasma:** Plasma, the yellowish liquid part of your blood, carries special things called antibodies. These tiny soldiers zoom around your body and fight off germs that try to make you sick. It's like having a tiny army inside you, always ready to protect you!

~~~~~

Why did the bacteria go to the art museum?

Because it was "cultured!" 🤭

♤ **Bacteria:** Did you know that there are friendly bacteria called "Lactobacillus" that help us make yummy yogurt? These tiny helpers turn milk into yogurt by eating the sugars and producing acid, which thickens the milk and gives it a tangy taste.

Why did the germs start a podcast?
They wanted to "go viral!" 😎

👏 **Virus:** Some viruses change their outer layer, called a "capsid," to disguise themselves! This sneaky trick helps them hide from our body's defenders, the immune cells, making it a real-life game of hide and seek.

~~~~~

Why did the DNA go on a diet?
To fit into its "skinny-genes!" 😂

🧬 **DNA:** Every person has something called "genes" in their DNA that work like tiny artists mixing paint. These genes decide whether your hair will be black, brown, blonde, or red by choosing different amounts of these "paints" called eumelanin and pheomelanin.

~~~~~

What do biologists post on social media?
Mostly "cell-phies!" 😵

🔬 **Cells:** Did you know that the smallest cells in the world are so tiny that millions of them can fit on the tip of a needle? These microscopic cells belong to a type of bacteria known as "Mycoplasma." Some biologists use super powerful microscopes just to see them!

ANSWER KEY 8

```
U  N  E  R  Y  B  P  I  R  X  X  G
D  X (E  Y  E  B  A  L  L) Q  A  N
A  L  O  M  E (S  T  O  M  A  C  H)
R  P  I  Y (B  A  C  T  E  R  I  A)
T  B (B  O  N  E  S) F  H  K  R  E
E  K (L  U  N  G  S) V  I  G  S
R  I (B  R  P  L  G  A  U  L
I  D  L  R  F  R  L  P  H  O  C  Z  C
E  N  K  E  D  A  H  Q  U  I  P  S
S  E  B  A  N  S  I  M  C  D  V  M
G  Y  K  P  A  M  B  N  Y  P  X  U
V  K  L  P  Y  A  Y  V  I  M  A  A
```

ARTERIES   BACTERIA   BONES
BRAIN   DNA   EYEBALL
HAIR   KIDNEY   LUNGS
MUCUS   PLASMA   STOMACH

What did one kidney say to the other?
"Urine good company!" 🤢

⚙ **Kidneys:** Your kidneys are like your body's cleaners. Every minute, they clean and filter about 1.5 liters of blood—that's almost an entire soda bottle! They don't use soap though. They use a special filtering system that catches all the tiny waste particles and gets rid of them by producing urine.

〰〰〰〰

What is the pancreas' favorite instrument?
The "gland-piano!" 😎

🏭 **Glands:** The pancreas is considered a gland because it works like a little factory, producing a special juice and a hormone called insulin. This hormone is like a key that opens the doors of your cells, letting sugar in to give them energy to play!

〰〰〰〰

What did the tooth say as the Dentist was leaving?
"Fill me in when you get back!" 😄

🦷 **Teeth:** Each type of tooth in your mouth has its own special name based on its job. The sharp teeth near the front are called "canines," and the big, flat teeth in the back of your mouth are called "molars" because they help you grind your food into tiny pieces.

I heard a terrible joke about saliva...
It left a "bad taste in my mouth." 😵

🫦 **Saliva:** Did you know that in just one day, your mouth makes enough saliva to fill two average-sized soda cans? That's right! Saliva is super important because it helps us taste our food, start digesting it, and keeps our mouths clean and comfortable.

〰〰〰

Did you hear about the eyeballs who joined the circus?
It was a "big spectacle!" 😵

👀 **Eyeball:** Did you know that your eyeballs are actually not perfectly round? They are slightly flattened in the front and back, kind of like how a basketball would look if you squished some of the air out of it!

〰〰〰

Why did the hair get upset with the comb?
It kept "brushing her off!" 😎

💇 **Hair:** Can you believe that every hair on your head is like a tiny spring? If you stretch a hair and then let it go, it will bounce back to its original shape. That's because hair is naturally super elastic!

CONGRATULATIONS!

You've completed the course and are now an official graduate of *Wisecrack Academy*.

CLAIM YOUR CERTIFICATE

WISECRACK ACADEMY

CLASS CLOWN AWARD

⚛ SCIENCE

This certificate hereby acknowledges:

_____

STUDENT NAME

as a 'total gas' in the subject of science.

_____

COMPLETION DATE

Wallace G.

DEAN OF STUDENTS

OUR STORY

👋 Hey readers! We are Kevin & Wally, a father-son duo from a small lake community in the Pine Barrens of New Jersey. While I, Kevin, have previously published a book on marketing and the technology industry, it was far too "boring" for 6-year-old Wally to read and appreciate.

It was for this reason that we put our heads together to co-author a book that we both could enjoy and be proud of. This led to many nights of 15 minute "work sessions" as we came up with topics, wrote funny jokes, researched facts, worked with illustrators, ate snacks, and did whatever we had to do to keep the project going.

While this took almost a year to complete, we learned a lot and had a ton of fun together in the process. Even though the primary purpose of this book is to make you laugh and teach you about our favorite subject (science), we also hope that it inspires you to always try cool new things, no matter how difficult they may seem.

Kevin *Wally*

If you would like to reach out to us to say hello, or for other business inquiries, email: **books@kevinclune.com**

Made in the USA
Middletown, DE
16 November 2023